The Aboriginal American, Target of The Doctrine Of Discovery

Presented by

Meru El Muad'Dib

AMER'ICAN, noun A native of **America**; originally applied to the **aboriginals**, or **copper-colored** races, found here by the Europeans; but now applied to the descendants of Europeans born in **America**. 1828 Webster's Dictionary

Blood is in the soil, soil is in the blood

What is the most common blood type for black people?

Types **O** negative and **O positive** are in high demand. Only 7% of the population are **O** negative. However, the need for **O** negative blood is the highest because it is used most often during emergencies. The need for **O+** is high because it is the most frequently occurring blood type (37% of the population).

Google.com

The most common blood type in the U.S. is **O-positive**. About 37% of Caucasian people, **47% of African Americans**, 53% of Latin Americans, and 39% of Asian Americans have this blood type, according to The Red Cross. Type A-positive comes in second, and B-positive is third most common.

Google.com

Different racial and ethnic groups typically see a different distribution. For instance, 45 percent of Caucasians are **type O**, but **51 percent of African-Americans** and 57 percent of Hispanics are **type O**, according to the Red Cross. Google.com

	Caucasian	African-American	Latino-American	Asian
O +	37%	47%	53%	39%
O -	8%	4%	4%	1%
A +	33%	24%	29%	27%
A -	7%	2%	2%	0.5%
B +	9%	18%	9%	25%
B -	2%	1%	1%	0.4%
AB +	3%	4%	2%	7%
AB -	1%	0.3%	0.2%	0.1%

Google.com

African-American blood donors hold the power to save other African-American's in need of a blood transfusion. That's because donors with genetically-similar blood are more likely to be a match for patients from the same ethnic background.

When it comes to blood donations, researchers have found that African-Americans are under-represented among donors, and that minority donors in general are less likely to become regular donors.

https://www.google.com/search?ei=_bifXNjhGYaiswX3lrK4BA&q=native+american+o+blood+type&oq=native&gs_l=psy-ab.1.0.35i39l2j0i20i263j0i67l7.13271.17772..20005...12.0..0.117.1413.17j1....3..0....1..gws-wiz.....6..0i71j0j0i131j0i131i20i263j0i131i67.YjCzlBFkHJs

All major ABO blood alleles are found in most populations worldwide, whereas the majority of Native Americans are nearly exclusively in the O group. O allele molecular characterization could aid in elucidating the possible causes of group O predominance in Native American populations.

file://profiles-svr/RedirectedFolders/dhudson/Desktop/New%20Book%20ish/Blood_group_O_alleles_in_Native_American%20(1).pdf

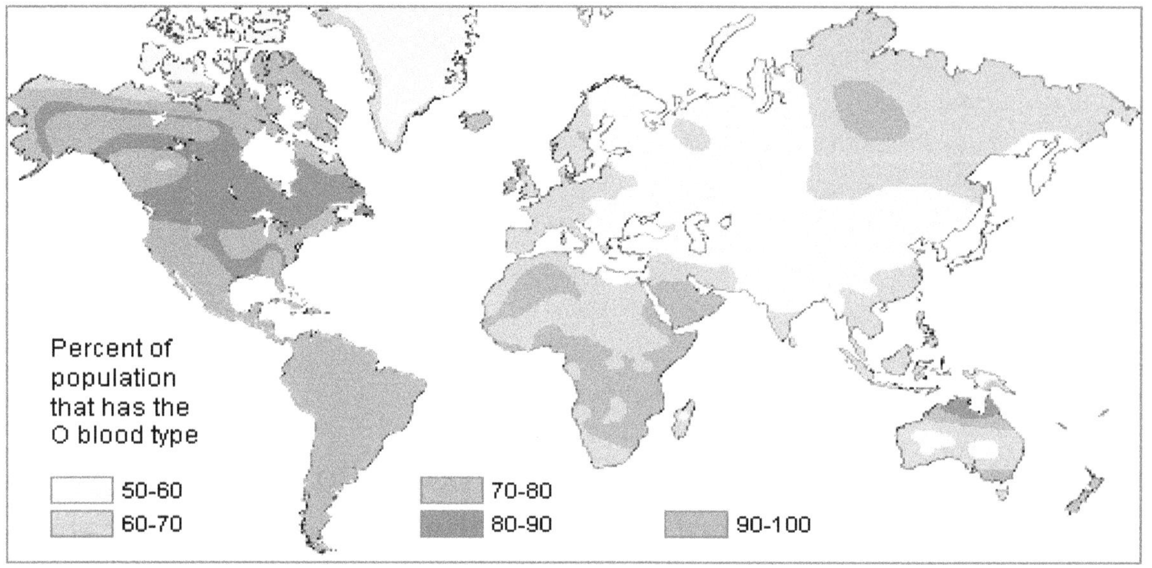

All of South America and the western half of the U.S. are type O.

As well as the southeast portion of the country where the Five Civilized Tribes lived.

How many slaves were brought to North America?

Did you know that **less than 10 percent of all African slaves actually came to North America**? So what was the percentage that came and why so few? Where did the rest go?

It's common to think that all black slaves came to what is now the United States. Since you're probably from here, and have been subject to the traditional school system, you may not have been taught otherwise. It's easy to get turned around by "word of mouth." However, black history facts indicate differently.

Over the course of three centuries, **African slaves in South America amassed over 90 percent of those taken from their homelands**. To put that in a numerical perspective, it's recorded that approximately 10.5 out of the recorded 12.5 million taken actually made it across the Atlantic Ocean without dying.

As is reported by the Gilder Lehrman Institute of American History, **six percent of these black slaves were taken to North America**. Only six percent.

https://www.inquisitr.com/1830533/black-history-less-than-10-percent-of-slaves-actually-came-to-north-america-transatlantic-slave-trade-where-did-they-all-go/

Fewer than **350,000** enslaved people were imported into the Thirteen Colonies and the U.S., constituting less than 5% of the twelve million enslaved people brought from Africa to the Americas. **The great majority of enslaved Africans were transported to sugar colonies in the Caribbean and to Brazil**.

Google.com

Well over 90 percent of enslaved Africans were imported into the Caribbean and South America. Only **about 6 percent of African captives were sent directly to British North America**. Yet by 1825, the US had a quarter of blacks in the New World.

https://www.gilderlehrman.org/content/historical-context-facts-about-slave-trade-and-slavery

The most comprehensive analysis of shipping records over the course of the slave trade is the **Trans-Atlantic Slave Trade Database**, edited by professors David Eltis and David Richardson. (**While the editors are careful to say that all of their figures are estimates**, **I believe that they are the best estimates that we have**, the proverbial "gold standard" in the field of the study of the slave trade.) Between 1525 and 1866, in the entire history of the slave trade to the New World, according to the Trans-Atlantic Slave Trade Database, 12.5 *million* Africans were shipped to the New World. 10.7 million survived the dreaded Middle Passage, disembarking in North America, the Caribbean and South America.

And how many of these 10.7 million Africans were shipped directly to North America? *Only about 388,000.* That's right: a tiny percentage.

In fact, **the overwhelming percentage of the African slaves were shipped directly to the Caribbean and South America; Brazil received *4.86 million Africans alone*!** Some scholars estimate that another 60,000 to 70,000 Africans ended up in the United States after touching down in the Caribbean first, so that would bring the total to **approximately *450,000* Africans who arrived in the United States over the course of the slave trade**.

https://www.theroot.com/how-many-slaves-landed-in-the-us-1790873989

Perhaps you, like me, were raised essentially to think of the slave experience primarily in terms of our black ancestors here in the United States. In other words, slavery was primarily about *us,* right, from Crispus Attucks and Phillis Wheatley, Benjamin Banneker and Richard Allen, all the way to Harriet Tubman, Sojourner Truth and Frederick Douglass. Think of this as an instance of what we might think of as *African-American exceptionalism.* (In other words, if it's in "the black Experience," it's got to be about black Americans.) Well, think again.
The most comprehensive analysis of shipping records over the course of the slave trade is the Trans-Atlantic Slave Trade Database, edited by professors David Eltis and David Richardson. (While the editors are careful to say that **all of their figures are estimates**, **I believe that they are the best estimates that we have,** the proverbial "gold standard" in the field of the study of the

slave trade.) Between 1525 and 1866, in the entire history of the slave trade to the New World, according to the Trans-Atlantic Slave Trade Database, 12.5 *million* Africans were shipped to the New World. 10.7 million survived the dreaded Middle Passage, disembarking in North America, the Caribbean and South America.
And how many of these 10.7 million Africans were shipped directly to North America? *Only about 388,000.* That's right: a tiny percentage. https://www.theroot.com/how-many-slaves-landed-in-the-us-1790873989

Did you know **that less than 10 percent of all African slaves actually came to North America**? So what was the percentage that came and why so few? Where did the rest go?

It's common to think that all black slaves came to what is now the United States. Since you're probably from here, and have been subject to the traditional school system, you may not have been taught otherwise. It's easy to get turned around by "word of mouth." However, black history facts indicate differently.

https://www.inquisitr.com/1830533/black-history-less-than-10-percent-of-slaves-actually-came-to-north-america-transatlantic-slave-trade-where-did-they-all-go/

When discussing slavery in America, it's important to look at the numbers. Some experts **estimate** that during the slave trade to the New World, more than 12.5 million people were stolen from Africa between 1525 and 1866. Of those who traveled the treacherous journey, only 10.7 million survived the Middle Passage.

Most captives were shipped directly to the **Caribbean** and **South America**, including **4.8 million to Brazil**, according to **Trans-Atlantic Slave Trade Database**.

But amazingly, only **388,000** were shipped directly to **North America**.

However, one number in particular, **20**, **signifies the start of slavery in the United States**. The first Africans to land in the British colony of **Jamestown**, **Virginia in 1619 were recorded as "20 and odd Negroes**."

Originating from Angola, these slaves were stolen from a Portuguese slave ship, then transported to an English warship flying a Dutch flag, and were eventually sold to colonial settlers.

Although slavery had no legal standing in the young colony at the time, **these 20 Africans were either kept as indentured servants or enslaved**, **introducing black chattel slavery into what is now the United States of America**.

Little information is known about the first 20, but the concept developed into institutional slavery, rapidly spreading throughout American colonies. By the time Abraham Lincoln issued the Emancipation Proclamation in 1863, **those "20 and odd Negroes" had mushroomed to 4 million slaves in America**.

https://www.ajc.com/lifestyles/1619-the-first-africans-arrive-the-new-world/ymhFu5bczYAUjPLDBX4mnK/

When it comes to the study of the slave trade, it is important to point out that **all the numbers are estimates**. They go on to say that out of all the estimated numbers, they believe (they don't know) these are the best estimates. The system for counting the number of slaves that left Africa and arrived here on the North American shores is flawed. It cannot be known. But they do know that the lowest amount arrived here in comparison with Brazil and the Caribbean.

The question must be asked, if African slaves were first recorded as arriving in North America in 1619, **who were the "slaves" between the time of Columbus (1492) until 1619**? That was 127 years. Who were the dark or copper colored skin people that were doing the work? Add to that, slaves (blacks, negroes, colored) in 1787 were counted as three-fifths of a person. How many people are we really talking about?

The entire system of counting and keeping track of the number of African slaves cannot be trusted. Take a look at what the census states:

The Federal Population Schedules, 1790–1840
Only the heads of free households appear in these records. All others, including slaves, are noted statistically under the head of household or reported owner.

This is from the National Archive and Records Administration. It goes on to say further down in the same document:

Slaves in the 1790--1840 **Census no notation of slave by name, age, sex, or origination appears**. **The census lists slaves statistically under the owner's name**.
https://www.archives.gov/files/research/census/african-american/census-1790-1930.pdf

Originally they didn't count slaves as individuals. Why would they when they weren't considered human? Then in 1787, they were counted as three fifths of a person which was for tax and legislative purposes, not for the census. The bottom line is, the numbers don't add up. The belief that none of those "four million" slaves were not reclassified Aboriginal Americans cannot be ignored. The fact that the Aboriginal Americans were re-labeled as "Indians," "black," "colored," "mulatto," "Negro," "octaroons," "quadroons," and any other slave label was proven in the previous volume.

Information on the Declaration

At this point let's take a look at one of the most sacred documents in European American history, the Declaration of Independence. Most have never read the document in full. Many read the first few lines as a tribute to democracy and justice for every citizen. Let's examine this document further.

The most sacred document wherein the U.S. celebrates its Fourth of July holiday, the Declaration of Independence, is known for having some of the most revolutionary words in history in regards to the equality of men who at the time had been forever accustomed to having caste-like systems whether it be Empires, noblemen and serfs, or a monarchy rule the American colonialists lived under.

After a brief introduction, the Declaration of Independence states in the eloquent prose of the Thomas Jefferson, "We hold these Truths to be self-evident, that all Men are created equal, that they are endowed by their Creator with certain unalienable Rights, that among these are Life, Liberty, and the Pursuit of Happiness."

Powerful words, indeed, and ones we should hold dear no matter where we are from or live. But if one reads through the document completely – as it's done annually and publicly in countless U.S. locations – it lists "repeated injuries and usurpations" and "tyranny" acts against the colonialists on behalf of King George III of Great Britain. The second paragraph concludes, "To prove this, let Facts be submitted to a candid world," before a list of 27 sentences listing various transgressions from tax complaints to forced military conscription.

The last of these complaints, however, is one that reads: He has excited domestic insurrections amongst us, and has endeavored to bring on the inhabitants of our frontiers, the **merciless Indian savages**, whose known rule of warfare, is undistinguished destruction of all ages, sexes and conditions.

Pause right there. Does the most famous document in American history really state "all Men are created equal," then hypocritically proclaim right afterward its first inhabitants are "**merciless Indian savages**"?

Yes, it really does, and this founding document was more than just a document written in the context of a bitter conflict. Consider, although Jefferson is most credited for penning this famous document, it was written by a committee of 5 people – including Benjamin Franklin and John Adams – and ratified 86 times by the Continental Congress before becoming official and signed. So this was a carefully mulled over phrase in that Natives would forever be considered "savages" in regards to their future relations with the U.S. https://newsmaven.io/indiancountrytoday/archive/the-declaration-of-independence-except-for-indian-savages-VeebEvQSV0as6vTpg8_5xg/

These so called mercilles indian savages were Aboriginal Americans defending their land. In today's political climate, those words would be considered hate speech. This is a highly celebrated and respected document, let that sink in.

The Island of Sincere Fiction

GOREE ISLAND, Senegal - Standing in a narrow doorway opening onto the Atlantic Ocean, tour guide Aladji Ndiaye asked a visitor to this Senegalese island's Slave House to imagine the millions of shackled Africans who stepped through it, forced onto overcrowded ships that would carry them to lives of slavery in the Americas.

"After walking through the door, it was bye-bye, Africa," said Ndiaye, pausing before solemnly pointing to the choppy waters below. "Many would try to escape. Those who did died. It was better we give ourselves to the sharks than be slaves."

This portal - called the "door of no return" - is one of the most powerful symbols of the Atlantic slave trade, serving as a backdrop for high-profile visits to Africa by Pope John Paul II, President Bill Clinton and President George W. Bush and a destination for thousands of African-Americans in search of their roots.

More than 200,000 people travel to this rocky island off the coast of Dakar each year to step inside the dark, dungeon-like holding rooms in the pink stucco Slave House and hear details of how 20 million slaves were chained and fattened for export here. Many visitors are moved to tears.

But whatever its emotional or spiritual power, **Goree Island's real role in the slave trade remains a matter of dispute**, **a contest between history and the power of myth**.

Despite the claims by Senegal's tour guides and tourism industry, **Goree Island was never a major shipping point for slaves, say historians**. **No slaves were ever sold at what is known as the "House of Slaves." No Africans ever stepped through the famous "door of no return" to waiting ships**, **either**.

"The whole story is phony," says Philip D. Curtin, a retired professor of history at the Johns Hopkins University who has written more than two dozen books on Atlantic slave trade and African history.

First used as stopover by Portuguese sailors in the 15th century, Goree Island was bought for a few iron nails by the Dutch before being seized by the French and the British.

Although it functioned as a commercial center, it was never a key departure point for slaves, Curtin says. **Most Africans sold into slavery in the Senegal region would have departed from thriving slave depots at the mouths of the Senegal River to the north and the Gambia River to the south**, he says.

During about 400 years of the Atlantic slave trade when an estimated 10 million Africans were taken from Africa, **maybe 50,000 slaves - not 20 million as claimed by the Slave House curator** - might have spent time on the island, Curtin says.

Even then, they would not have been locked in chains in the House of Slaves, Curtin says. Built in 1775-1778 by a wealthy merchant, **it was one of the most beautiful homes on the island**; it would not have been used as a warehouse for slaves other than those who might have been owned by the merchant.

Likewise, Curtin adds, **the widely accepted story that the "door of no return" was the final departure point for millions of slaves is not true**. There are too many rocks to allow boats to dock safely and a beach nearby that would have been the easiest place for loading ships, he says.

Curtin's assessment is widely shared by historians, including Abdoulaye Camara, curator of the Goree Island Historical Museum, which is a 10-minute walk from the Slave House.

The Slave House, says Camara, **offers a distorted account of the island's history - created with tourists in mind**.... https://historynewsnetwork.org/blog/5969

President Obama visited one of Africa's most famous memorials to the slave trade on Thursday, the House of Slaves on Senegal's Goree Island. The official story is that millions of African slaves passed through the house's Door of No Return, which faces West across the Atlantic; countless visitors have come to contemplate the slave trade and to pay heartfelt tribute, including Nelson Mandela, Pope John Paul II and the last three U.S. presidents.

Except that the official story turns out to be largely a myth. **Historians have agreed since the 1990s that the house was likely just a private residence that had nothing to do with the slave trade**. Earlier, **we explored this long-standing disconnect between the reality and myth of Goree Island**, why it's proven so resilient and what it says about the world's struggle to deal with this dark chapter in history.

University of Chicago historical anthropologist Francois Richard, a West Africa scholar who has studied the slave trade, has some thoughts about that disconnect between the myth and reality of Goree. Richard emphasizes the house's value as a sort of manifestation of slavery's legacy, which is still so big today that it demands this sort of totem. He reproduces a term that seems to capture the phenomenon well: it is a "**sincere fiction**." Here's Richard:

1) Yes, there has been heated academic debate around Goree, but in the mid-90s(following a controversial article written in 1996 in Le Monde). The debates have largely been on the revisionist side, and most historians today would

argue that the scale of the slave trade in Goree was likely much lower than in many other parts of western Africa (for a variety of reasons. I should note, however, that turning the question of international slavery into a statistical exercise is not the most useful way to think about it, and sadly that legacy has clouded academic debates more than it has helped). So, Goree was a transit point, though the volume of trade there was 'fairly' low (square quotes are important here) and that it ebbed and flowed over time, probably decreasing over time, especially after the 1500s. as captives were increasingly retained in Senegal to work in food production.

2) Yes, there was slavery on the island, but of a much different kind than the chattel slavery that was established on plantations in the Caribbean and Americas.

3) The House of Slaves holds a huge amount of symbolic value as a 'place of memory,' a testimony to a not-so-savory part of global history. In this sense, the house was erected into a 'myth' (or perhaps, a term I'd prefer, to follow sociologist Pierre Bourdieu, a sincere fiction) and mobilized as a memento.

As far as archives will go, the house was built probably in the 1700s, thus rather late in the era of the Atlantic trade, at a point when the commerce in slaves was diminishing and when the gum trade was gaining ascendance. What's more, it was a residential structure, upper floor were living quarters, lower sections were probably for merchandise and magazine. And yes, the enslaved people living there were probably attached to the house (cooks, domestics, laborers, traders, etc.).

Some people use the history/memory couplet to parse the problem of Goree's house of slaves (i.e., history concerned with facts and memory with symbolic value and historical gravity, a mode of affective resonance absolutely central to identities in the African diaspora). It's not the most satisfying or cutting was of analyzing the phenomenon, but it has a merit of offering a point of entry. What's important to remember, though, is that while the details about the house may not be entirely exact, they do speak to a deeper historical truth - namely, the experience and infamy of turning humanity into a commodity. https://www.washingtonpost.com/news/worldviews/wp/2013/07/01/the-sincere-fiction-of-goree-island-africas-best-known-slave-trade-memorial/?noredirect=on&utm_term=.a31b133bb898

Gorée Island is listed on the UNESCO world heritage list. On the UNESCO website, we can read that "from the 15th to the 19th century, it was the largest slave-trading centre on the African coast." The BBC and The New York Times have both claimed that millions of slaves had been held here. Celebrities like Pope John Paul II, Nelson Mandela, and multiple US presidents, as well as (according to Wikipedia) 200 000 visitors every year, have visited not only Gorée Island but also its House of Slaves. Judging by Trip Advisor reviews, most, like me, come to the island under the impression that Gorée really did play a major role in the trans-Atlantic slave trade, and the House of Slaves really did house slaves waiting to be exported.

Other sources paint a completely different picture. The Telegraph quotes historian Ralph Austen:

There are literally no historians who believe the Slave House is what they're claiming it to be, or that believe Goree was statistically significant in terms of the slave trade.

Philip Curtin's statistical analysis of documentation of trans-Atlantic voyages suggests that no more than 300 slaves departed from Goree each year. Similar numbers appear to be backed up by the Du Bois Institute's Trans-Atlantic Slave Trade Database (as reported and further backed up here).

When this data was publicized in a 1996 article in the French press, Senegalese historians were outraged. Here's historian Mbaye Gueye:

It is true that the slave trade has never been among the preoccupations of European historians, but this was nothing less than an attempt to falsify the past. There are evidently still people who simply wish to absolve themselves of this past.

Mbaye Gueye claimed to have more than ad hominem attacks up his sleeve—he apparently found "original archives from the French port of Nantes that showed that between 1763 and 1775 alone one port had traded more than 103,000 slaves from Goree" (the quote is from the same NYT article.)

This is the one (initially) solid-looking piece of evidence I've been able to find for the Gorée-as-slave-trade-center theory—but even this crumbles under scrutiny. In a footnote in this article, we read that the numbers in the Nantes records were for trades brought in from all of West Africa. Gorée isn't mentioned in them at all.

As far I've been able to verify, then, Gorée was hardly the slave-trading center that UNESCO makes it out to be. As to the so-called Slave House, it was:

- in the area of the island populated by rich free people (and, sometimes, their domestic slaves),

- facing out to a treacherous part of the coast that ships probably wouldn't have departed from,
- built after the zenith of the slave trade.

Not every horrific slave story is a true story.

If the House of Slaves wasn't a holding pen for America-bound slaves, what *was* it? The house, built around 1776, belonged to the Pépins, a family of rich merchants of mixed Afro-European descent.

The most famous member of the family, Anne Pépin, was the mistress of Senegal's French governor Stanislas de Boufflers, who according to Wikipedia "attempted to mitigate the horrors of the slave trade." Anne Pépin was one of the so-called "Signares:" African and Afro-European women who had formed relationship with powerful white male invaders, and who often worked as merchants and owned land and slaves.[2]

What should we think of the Signares? Were they feminist icons, black women who managed to wield considerable power in an era where that would have hardly seemed possible? Or femmes fatales who used their sex appeal to their advantage and didn't shy away from the slave trade, buying and selling their own kinsmen? Were they the victims of the lust and power of male European invaders, who eloped with them only to leave them behind and sail off to Europe, often back to the wives they had left behind? Were they just making the best of an awful situation, using their influence to ensure better treatment of their partners' domestic slaves—or were they heedless of the suffering they contributed to, driven by the pursuit of wealth and power?

The answer may well be: all of the above. The human soul is a complex place—but that doesn't bring in tourists. Can you blame the people of Senegal for not broadcasting the story of these mixed-race slave-owning badass island ladies? Can you blame them for, instead, feeding visitors the thrillingly familiar story of easily condemnable atrocities hidden in the dungeons of a pastel town? After all, the House of Slaves is Senegal's top tourist destination, and its historically inaccurate story has forty years of bestseller status speaking in its favor.

Anne Pépin and her family didn't keep slaves waiting to be shipped across the Atlantic—**those were held in a fortress on the other side of the island**—but they probably did own so-called indigenous slaves: people kept on the island by force for domestic labor. (It was most likely indigenous slaves who built the Slave House and many other Gorée buildings.) This is another part of the Gorée story that isn't often told: by the eighteenth century, over half of the island's population consisted of indigenous slaves. The mistreatment these people endured was just slight enough for us to have erased it from our collective memory.

The "cells" of the House of Slaves, then, were probably the lodgings of indigenous slaves, whose lot, though certainly not enviable, didn't feature the shackles now exhibited here.

And the Door of No Return? We don't know for sure, but it may have been… a garbage dump for throwing waste into the sea. (Take this with a grain of salt; the reference is from the UK's The Daily Mail, which isn't exactly famous for stellar journalism…)

The whole story about the horrors of the House of Slaves seems to have originated with a single person: **curator Boubacar Joseph Ndiaye. For forty years, right up to his death at 86, he led daily tours of the house, telling his gory and compelling tale to transfixed audiences**.

During those forty years, the House of Slaves and its Door of No Return acquired a cult status. Members of the African diaspora would come here to come to terms with what their ancestors had lived through. (Those who come from the United States are especially unlikely to be retracing their ancestors' footsteps; **the slaves who did pass through Gorée were overwhelming shipped to Europe and South America.**)

Since Ndiaye's death, no one has been proclaiming the myth of Gorée quite so forcefully. More and more visitors are aware of the controversy surrounding the House of Slaves; it's right there in the Wikipedia article. The Bradt Guide to Senegal cites both the Phil Curtin numbers and the alleged Nantes document, diplomatically concluding "The true numbers may never be known." In other words: "**we don't want to anger anyone**."

A sign outside the door to the House of Slaves stamped "UNESCO" informs you that the site is "under renovation" to bring it up to 21st century museum standards. There's no explanation of this mysterious phrase, no grand retraction of the House of Slave's claim to fame—but the museum is slowly ceasing to be a memorial to the invented horrors of the building it's housed in and turning into a monument to the very real horrors of the entire trans-Atlantic slave trade.

Slowly but surely, Gorée is turning into a symbol. I wish UNESCO openly acknowledged that they'd made a mistake, rather than quietly filing away old signs—but at least the end destination is a noble one. I don't want people to stop coming here. This tiny, remarkably preserved island is uniquely placed to play the role of an anchor for the imagination.

Ndiaye didn't really *invent* the story of the House of Slaves; he simply *relocated* a true story to this tiny island. The shackles exhibited here weren't used in this house—but they were certainly used during the horrific forced journey across the Atlantic so many had to endure. Gorée wasn't the main location of the slave trade—there were *many* places like it, each with its trickle of atrocities.

In fact, there is a **true "door of no return" west of the Atlantic: South Carolina's Sullivan's Island**, the site of a checkpoint and quarantine house for 40% of the slaves shipped into British North America. Today, Sullivan's Island is a wealthy beach resort town, with some of the highest real estate prices in the area.

There is a House of Slaves in Gorée for exactly the same reasons for which there isn't one in Sullivan's Island: political convenience and monetary gains.

You visit Sullivan's Island to sunbathe—or to bask in the glory of the American victory which took place there in 1776. You visit Gorée to feel bad—about what you already know.
https://medium.com/@insensified/between-scam-and-symbol-9ed57ac8dce0

Despite the claims by Senegal's tour guides and tourism industry, Goree Island was never a major shipping point for slaves, historians say. **No slaves were ever sold at what is known as the House of Slaves**, they insist. **No Africans ever stepped through the infamous Door of No Return to waiting ships**.

"**The whole story is phony**," said Philip Curtin, a retired professor of history at Johns Hopkins University who has written more than two dozen books on the Atlantic slave trade and African history.

First used as a stopover by Portuguese sailors in the 15th Century, Goree Island was bought for a few iron nails by the Dutch before being seized by the French and the British.

Although it functioned as a commercial center, it was never a key departure point for slaves, Curtin said. Most Africans sold into slavery in the Senegal region would have departed from thriving slave depots at the mouths of the Senegal River to the north and the Gambia River to the south, he said.

During about 400 years of the Atlantic slave trade when an estimated 10 million Africans were taken from Africa, maybe 50,000 slaves--not 20 million as claimed by the House of Slaves' curator--might have spent time on the island, Curtin said.

Even then, **they would not have been locked in chains in the House of Slaves**, Curtin said. Built in 1775-1778 by a wealthy merchant, it was one of the most beautiful homes on the island; it would not have been used as a warehouse for slaves other than those who might have been owned by the merchant.

Likewise, Curtin added, **the widely accepted story that the Door of No Return was the final departure point for millions of slaves is not true**. There are too many rocks to allow boats to dock safely, he said.

Curtin's assessment is widely shared by historians, including Abdoulaye Camara, curator of the Goree Island Historical Museum, a 10-minute walk from the House of Slaves.

The House of Slaves, said Camara, **offers a distorted account of the island's history and was created with tourists in mind**.

No one is quite sure where the House of Slaves got its name, but Camara and Curtin credit Boubacar Joseph Ndiaye, the House of

Slaves' curator since the 1960s, with promoting it as a tourist attraction.

Boubacar Joseph Ndiaye is famous in Senegal for offering thousands of visitors chilling details of the squalid conditions of the slaves' holding cells, the chains used to shackle them and the walk through the door of no return.

Tour guide vs. historian

"Joseph Ndiaye offers a strong, powerful, sentimental history. I am a historian. I am not allowed to be sentimental," Camara said.

But Camara said he thinks Ndiaye has played an important role in **offering the descendents of slaves an emotional shrine to commemorate the sacrifices of their ancestors**.

"**The slaves did not pour through that door**. **The door is a symbol**. **The history and memory needs to have a strong symbol,**" he said. "You either accept it or you don't accept it. It's difficult to interpret a symbol."

When historians have questioned the significance of the island and the House of Slaves, they have been met with accusations of revisionism. http://www.chicagotribune.com/news/ct-xpm-2004-07-27-0407270330-story.html

Aboriginal American slavery (Indian)

Carolinas

Further information: Colonial period of South Carolina

Until the early 18th century, enslaved **Africans were difficult to acquire in the colonies that became the United States**, as **most were sold to the West Indies**, **where the large plantations and high mortality rates required continued**

importation of slaves. One of the first major centers of African slavery in the English North American colonies occurred with the founding of Charles Town and the Province of Carolina in 1670. The colony was founded mainly by planters from the overpopulated British sugar island of Barbados, who brought relatively large numbers of African slaves from that island to establish new plantations.

For several decades it was difficult for planters north of the Caribbean to acquire African slaves. To meet agricultural labor needs, colonists practiced **Indian slavery** for some time. **The Carolinians transformed the Indian slave trade during the late 17th and early 18th centuries by treating such slaves as a trade commodity to be exported, mainly to the West Indies**. Historian Alan Gallay estimates that between 1670 and 1715, **between 24,000 and 51,000 captive Native Americans were exported from South Carolina**—much more than the number of Africans imported to the colonies of the future United States during the same period.

New England

Slaves, African and **Native American**, made up a smaller part of the New England economy, which was based on yeoman farming and trades, and a smaller fraction of the population, but they were present. **The Puritans codified slavery** in 1641. The Massachusetts royal colony passed the *Body of Liberties*, which prohibited slavery in some instances, but did allow three legal bases of slavery. Slaves could be held if they were captives of war, if they sold themselves into slavery, were purchased from elsewhere, or if they were sentenced to slavery by the governing authority. The Body of Liberties used the word "strangers" to refer to people bought and sold as slaves, as they were generally not English subjects. Colonists came to equate this term **with Native Americans** and Africans.

https://en.wikipedia.org/wiki/Slavery_in_the_colonial_United_States

Remember, New England is north of the Mason-Dixon line.

The record of Native enslavement also shows how the white desire to put workers in bondage **intensified the chaos of contact**, **disrupting intertribal politics** and **creating uncertainty and instability among people already struggling to adapt to a radically new balance of power**.

Before looking at the way Native enslavement happened on the local level (really the only way to approach a history this fragmented and various), it helps to appreciate the sweep of the phenomenon. How common was it for Indians to be enslaved by Euro-Americans? Counting can be difficult, because many instances of Native enslavement in the Colonial period were illegal or ad hoc and left no paper trail. But historians have tried. A few of their estimates: Thousands of Indians were enslaved in Colonial New England, according to Margaret Ellen Newell. Alan Gallay writes that between 1670 and 1715**, more Indians were exported into slavery through Charles Town (now Charleston, South Carolina) than Africans were imported**. Brett Rushforth recently attempted a tally of the total numbers of enslaved, and he told me that **he thinks 2 million to 4 million indigenous people in the Americas, North and South, may have been enslaved over the centuries that the practice prevailed**—a much larger number than had previously been thought.

"It's not on the level of the African slave trade," which brought 10 million people to the Americas, but the earliest history of the European colonies in the Americas is marked by Native bondage. "If you go up to about 1680 or 1690 there still, by that period, had been more enslaved Indians than enslaved Africans in the Americas."

http://www.slate.com/articles/news_and_politics/cover_story/2016/01/native_american_slavery_historians_uncover_a_chilling_chapter_in_u_s_history.html

Slave Voyage index

History of the Project

A glance at the Sources section of “Understanding the Database” establishes Voyages as the product of an international research endeavor that has ranged far beyond the labors of the current project team. From the late 1960s, **Herbert S. Klein** and other scholars began to collect archival data on slave-trading voyages **from unpublished sources** and to code them into a machine-readable format. In the 1970s and 1980s, **scholars created a number of slave ship datasets**, several of which the current authors chose to recode from the primary sources rather than integrate the datasets of those scholars into the present set. By the late 1980s, there were records of approximately 11,000 individual trans-Atlantic voyages in sixteen separate datasets, **not all of which were trans-Atlantic**, **nor**, **as it turned out**, **slave voyages**. And of course, some sets overlapped others. Several listings of voyages extracted from more than one source had appeared in hard copy form, notably three volumes of voyages from French ports published by Jean Mettas and Serge and Michelle Daget and two volumes of Bristol voyages (expanded to four by 1996) authored by David Richardson. The basis for each dataset was usually the records of a specific European nation or the particular port where slaving voyages originated, with the information available reflecting the nature of the records that had survived rather than the structure of the voyage itself. Scholars of the slave trade spent the first quarter century of the computer era working largely in **isolation**, each using one source only as well as a separate format, though the Curtin, Mettas, and Richardson collections were early exceptions to this pattern.

https://slavevoyages.org/about/about

Decision In St. Louis

In 1846, Scott sued for his freedom on the grounds that he had lived in a free state and a free territory for a prolonged period of time. Finally, after eleven years, his case reached the Supreme Court. At stake were answers to critical questions, including slavery in the territories and citizenship of African-Americans. The verdict was a bombshell.

- The Court ruled that Scott's "sojourn" of two years to Illinois and the Northwest Territory did not make him free once he returned to Missouri.
- The Court further ruled that **as a black man Scott was excluded from United States citizenship** and **could not, therefore, bring suit**. According to the opinion of the Court, **African-Americans had not been part of the "sovereign people" who made the Constitution**.
- The Court also ruled that Congress never had the right to prohibit slavery in any territory. Any ban on slavery was a violation of the Fifth Amendment, which prohibited denying property rights without due process of law.
- The Missouri Compromise was therefore unconstitutional.

http://www.ushistory.org/us/32a.asp

Chief Justice Roger B. Taney wrote the majority decision, which was issued on March 6, 1857. The court held that **Scott was not free** based on his residence in either Illinois or Wisconsin **because he was not considered a person under the U.S. Constitution**–in the opinion of the justices, **black people were**

not considered citizens when the Constitution was **drafted in 1787**. According to Taney, Dred Scott was the property of his owner, and property could not be taken from a person without due process of law.

https://www.history.com/this-day-in-history/dred-scott-decision

There are two leading questions presented by the record:

1. Had the Circuit Court of the United States jurisdiction to hear and determine the case between these parties? And

2. If it had jurisdiction, is the judgment it has given erroneous or not?

The defendant pleaded in abatement to the jurisdiction of the court, that the plaintiff was not a citizen of the State of Missouri, as alleged in his declaration, **being a negro of African descent, whose ancestors were of pure African blood and who were brought into this country and sold as slaves**.

Before we speak of the pleas in bar, it will be proper to dispose of the questions which have arisen on the plea in abatement.

That plea denies the right of the plaintiff to sue in a court of the United States, for the reasons therein stated.

If the question raised by it is legally before us, and the court should be of opinion that the facts stated in it disqualify the plaintiff from becoming a citizen, in the sense in which that word is used in the Constitution of the United States, then the judgment of the Circuit Court is erroneous, and must be reversed.

The question is simply this: **can a negro whose ancestors were imported into this country and sold as slaves become a member of the political community formed and brought into**

existence by the Constitution of the United States, and as such become entitled to all the rights, and privileges, and immunities, guarantied by that instrument to the citizen, one of which rights is the privilege of suing in a court of the United States in the cases specified in the Constitution?

It will be observed that **the plea applies to that class of persons only whose ancestors were negroes of the African race, and imported into this country and sold and held as slaves**. The only matter in issue before the court, therefore, is, **whether the descendants of such slaves, when they shall be emancipated, or who are born of parents who had become free before their birth, are citizens of a State in the sense in which the word "citizen" is used in the Constitution of the United States**. And this being the only matter in dispute on the pleadings, the court must be understood as speaking in this opinion of that class only, that is, of those persons who are the descendants of Africans who were imported into this country and sold as slaves.

The situation of this population was altogether unlike that of the Indian race. The latter, it is true, formed no part of the colonial communities, and never amalgamated with them in social connections or in government. But although they were uncivilized, they were yet a free and independent people, associated together in nations or tribes and governed by their own laws. **Many of these political communities were situated in territories to which the white race claimed the ultimate right of dominion**. But that claim was acknowledged to be subject to the right of the Indians to occupy it as long as they thought proper, and neither the English nor colonial Governments claimed or exercised any dominion over the tribe or nation by whom it was occupied, nor claimed the right to the possession of the territory, until the tribe or nation consented to cede it. These Indian Governments were regarded and treated as foreign Governments as much so as if an ocean had separated the red man from the white, and their freedom has constantly been acknowledged, from the time of the first emigration to the English colonies to the present day, by the different Governments which succeeded each other. Treaties have been negotiated with them, and their alliance sought for in war, and **the people who compose these Indian political communities have always been treated as foreigners not living under our Government**. It is true that the course of events has brought the Indian tribes within the limits of the United States under subjection to the white race, and it has been found necessary, for their sake as well as our own, to regard them **as in a state of pupilage, and to legislate to a certain extent over them and the territory they occupy**. But they may, without doubt, like the subjects of any other foreign Government, **be naturalized by the authority of Congress, and become citizens of a State, and of the United States**, and if an individual should leave his nation or tribe and take up his abode among the white population, he would be entitled to all the rights and privileges which would belong to an emigrant from any other foreign people.

We proceed to examine the case as presented by the pleadings.

The words "people of the United States" and "citizens" are synonymous terms, and mean the same thing. They both describe the political body who, according to our republican institutions, form the sovereignty and who hold the power and conduct the Government through their representatives. They are what we familiarly call the "sovereign people," and every citizen is one of this people, and a constituent member of this sovereignty. The question before us is whether the class of persons described in the plea in abatement compose a portion of this people, and are constituent members of this sovereignty? **We think they are not**, **and that they are not included, and were not intended to be included**, **under the word "citizens" in the Constitution,**

and can therefore claim none of the rights and privileges which that instrument provides for and secures to citizens of the United States. On the contrary, they were at that time considered as a subordinate and inferior class of beings who had been subjugated by the dominant race, and, whether emancipated or not, yet remained subject to their authority, and had no rights or privileges but such as those who held the power and the Government might choose to grant them.

The question then arises, whether the provisions of the Constitution, in relation to the personal rights and privileges to which the citizen of a State should be entitled, embraced the negro African race, at that time in this country or who might afterwards be imported, who had then or should afterwards be made free in any State, and to put it in the power of a single State to make him a citizen of the United States and endue him with the full rights of citizenship in every other State without their consent? Does the Constitution of the United States act upon him whenever he shall be made free under the laws of a State, and raised there to the rank of a citizen, and immediately clothe him with all the privileges of a citizen in every other State, and in its own courts?

The court think the affirmative of these propositions cannot be maintained. And if it cannot, the plaintiff in error could not be a citizen of the State of Missouri within the meaning of the Constitution of the United States, and, consequently, was not entitled to sue in its courts.

It is true, every person, and every class and description of persons who were, at the time of the adoption of the Constitution, recognized as citizens in the several States became also citizens of this new political body, but none other; it was formed by them, and for them and their posterity, but for no one else. And the personal rights and privileges guarantied to citizens of this new sovereignty were intended to embrace those only who were then members of the several State communities, or who should afterwards by birthright or otherwise become members according to the provisions of the Constitution and the principles on which it was founded. It was the union of those who were at that time members of distinct and separate political communities into one political family, whose power, for certain specified purposes, was to extend over the whole territory of the United States. And it gave to each citizen rights and privileges outside of his State which he did not before possess, and placed him in every other State upon a perfect equality with its own citizens as to rights of person and rights of property; it made him a citizen of the United States.

It becomes necessary, therefore, to determine who were citizens of the several States when the Constitution was adopted. And in order to do this, we must recur to the Governments and institutions of the thirteen colonies when they separated from Great Britain and formed new sovereignties, and took their places in the family of independent nations. We must inquire who, at that time, were recognized as the people or citizens of a State whose rights and liberties had been outraged by the English Government, and who declared their independence and assumed the powers of Government to defend their rights by force of arms.

In the opinion of the court, the legislation and histories of the times, and the language used in the Declaration of Independence, **show that neither the class of persons who had been imported as slaves nor their descendants, whether they had become free or not, were then acknowledged as a part of the people, nor intended to be included in the general words used in that memorable instrument**.

They had for more than a century before been regarded as beings of an inferior order, and altogether unfit to associate

with the white race either in social or political relations, and **so far inferior that they had no rights which the white man was bound to respect**, **and that the negro might justly and lawfully be reduced to slavery for his benefit. He was bought and sold, and treated as an ordinary article of merchandise and traffic whenever a profit could be made by it. This opinion was at that time fixed and universal in the civilized portion of the white race**. It was regarded as an axiom in morals as well as in politics which no one thought of disputing or supposed to be open to dispute, and men in every grade and position in society daily and habitually acted upon it in their private pursuits, as well as in matters of public concern, without doubting for a moment the correctness of this opinion.

And in no nation was this opinion more firmly fixed or more uniformly acted upon than by the English Government and English people. They not only seized them on the coast of Africa and sold them or held them in slavery for their own use, but **they took them as ordinary articles of merchandise to every country where they could make a profit on them, and were far more extensively engaged in this commerce than any other nation in the world**.

The opinion thus entertained and acted upon in England was naturally impressed upon the colonies they founded on this side of the Atlantic. And, accordingly**, a negro of the African race was regarded by them as an article of property**, **and held**, **and bought and sold as such**, in every one of the thirteen colonies which united in the Declaration of Independence and afterwards formed the Constitution of the United States. The slaves were more or less numerous in the different colonies as slave labor was found more or less profitable. But no one seems to have doubted the correctness of the prevailing opinion of the time.

https://www.law.cornell.edu/supremecourt/text/60/393

It is not necessary to have read my first volume to understand what is going on. For those who haven't had the opportunity to read, '*The Truth of the Doctrine of Discovery*,' let us review. Catholic Popes issued papal bulls that determined how European nations would colonized the rest of the world. The popes said, **"to invade, search out, capture, vanquish, subdue, Saracens (Moors and Muslims)and pagans."** Also to **convert the people to his and their use and profit**. The latter part is what seen happening, their use and profit.

When they referred to the Aboriginal Americans as "ordinary articles of merchandise," and "make profit on them;" they are obeying the pope's papal bulls. That point must be grasped and understood by todays Aboriginal Americans. These are not random acts and attitudes they display towards us. This is part of an agenda that is hundreds of years old.

A Theory Is Not A Fact

Scientific evidence refuting the theory of modern humanity's African genesis is common knowledge among those familiar with the most recent scientific papers on the human Genome, Mitochondrial DNA and Y-chromosomes. Regrettably, within mainstream press and academia circles, there seems to be a conspicuous – and dare we say it – deliberate vacuum when it comes to reporting news of these recent studies and their obvious implications.

The whole 'Out of Africa' myth has its roots in the mainstream academic campaign in the 1990's to remove the concept of Race. When I did my degree they all spent a lot of time on the 'Out of Africa' thing but it's been completely disproved by genetics. Mainstream still hold on to it.

It did begin the early 90's. And the academics most responsible for cementing both the Out-of Africa theory and the complementary common ancestral African mother – given the name of "Eve" – in the public arena and nearly every curriculum, were **Professors Alan C. Wilson** and **Rebecca L. Cann**. In their defense, the authors of this paper were fully aware that genealogy is not in any way linked to geography, and that their placement of Eve in Africa was an assumption, never an assertion. In their seminal paper *The Recent African Genesis of Humans,* they even stipulated "that all humans today can be traced along maternal lines of descent to a woman who lived about 200,000 years ago, **probably** in Africa."

So how is it that their "**probably**" has morphed into our collective "**definitely**"?

Over time, even the two researchers came to discover that the research of Original Mitochondrial DNA was fundamentally flawed. Both separately conducted further tests on Mitochondrial DNA found within the blood of full-descent Original people, arriving at the same conclusion, **both recanted their previous assumptions by acknowledging that *Homo sapien sapiens* originated in Australia**.

Professor Alan Wilson came to Australia in 1987 and 1989 to personally supervise the collection of Original blood from a variety of locations throughout Australia. With a mutation rate of 70% from the samples analyzed, which is manifestly higher than any other race, Wilson was compelled to admit that:

> … it seems too far out to admit, but while *Homo erectus* was muddling along in the rest of the world, a few *erectus* had got to Australia and did something dramatically different – not even with stone tools – **but it is here that *Homo sapiens* emerged and evolved**.

Rebecca Cann was more expansive and specific in declaring that the Original "Mitochondrial DNA puts the origin of *Homo Sapiens* much further back and indicates that the Australian Aborigines arose 400,000 years ago from two distinct lineages, far earlier than any other racial group." The notions of a "far earlier" time frame when estimating *when*, and the existence of "two lineages" in Australia when grappling with *who,* are constant themes that can be found within many other reports investigating the make up of the genes and chromosomes of *Homo sapien sapiens*.

https://wakeup-world.com/2013/12/16/dna-evidence-debunks-the-out-of-africa-theory-of-human-evolution/

They were wrong and had the integrity to admit that mistake and tidy up the bad research and errors made.

"Australian scientists say analysis of the oldest DNA ever taken from skeletal remains challenges the theory that all modern humans can trace their recent ancestry to Africa.

What our evidence shows is that the situation is much more complicated than any of these supporters of Out of Africa would have imagined.

Before the beginning of the last decade of the twentieth century both Cann and Wilson had recanted and were certain that it was in **Australia**, not Africa, humanity came into existence.

They were wrong and had the integrity to admit that mistake and tidy up the bad research and errors made. Cann was the first to see the error of their ways and in a sampling of the blood of "112 humans, including twelve Australian Aborigines (sic), all from Western Australia." (65) She found that "mitochondrial DNA puts the origin of Homo sapiens much further back and indicates that the Australian Aborigines (sic) arose 400,000 years ago from two distinct lineages, far earlier than any other racial group."

https://thrivalinternational.com/2017/11/18/the-scientists-responsible-for-the-out-of-africa-theory-admit-they-were-wrong-are-we-even-listening/

The pros and cons of this issue can and probably will be argued for a very long time. One thing we must seriously consider is, the people who created the Out of Africa theory, said they made a mistake.

When Moors Look Like Aboriginal Americans (Indians)

CHAPTER 189 - SCHOOL IN INDIAN RIVER HUNDRED

AN ACT APPROPRIATING MONEY FOR THE PAYMENT OF THE SALARY OF THE TEACHER AT THE SCHOOL IN INDIAN RIVER HUNDRED, SUSSEX COUNTY, DELAWARE.

Be it enacted by the Senate and House of Representatives of the State of Delaware in General Assembly met:

Section 1. That Chapter 160, of Volume 32, Laws of Delaware, as amended by Chapter 222, Volume 36, Laws of Delaware, be and the same is hereby further amended by striking out all of the following sentence beginning in the 17th line of Section 1. of said Chapter 222, Volume 36, Laws of Delaware, reading as follows: "The State Board of Education may establish schools for children of people called **Moors**, which schools shall be free to all such children between the ages of six and twenty-one years, inclusive", and inserting in lieu thereof the following: "The State Board of Education shall establish schools for children of people called **Moors or Indians**, and if any **Moor or Indian** school is in existence or shall be hereafter established, the State Board of Education shall pay the salary of any teacher or teachers thereof, provided that the school is open for school sessions during the minimum number of days required by law for school attendance and provided further that such school shall be free to all children of the people called Moors, or the people called Indians, between the ages of six and twenty-one years."

Approved April 15, 1935.

http://delcode.delaware.gov/sessionlaws/ga105/chp189.shtml

The stupendous deserts between the Nueces and Bravo Rivers are the natural boundaries between the Anglo-Saxon and the **Mauritanian** races. There ends the valley of the west. There Mexico begins. Thence, beyond the Bravo, begin the **Moorish** people, and their **Indian associates**, to whom Mexico properly belongs;... The Old South Leaflets edited by Edwin Doak Mead 1/3/1845

That among the reputed ancestors of the **Aboriginal American Indian Population**, (Natives) are **Moors** and **Turks.** From a Federal Depository of New York State, in The Handbook of North American Indians pg. 290 – United States Government Printing Office, Washington D.C. 20402 Stock Number: 047-000-00351-2 Copyright © 1978 by Smithsonian Institution Library of Congress Cataloging in Publication

"It would stand to reason, that he [European colonists] stole the word **MOOR from the Indians so he could hide the true word for a Culture**, Language, a People and an Empire. If he did, it would have to be for DAMN GOOD REASON". Time Walkers by Meredith Musa Quinn ["Dakota" Indian]

"One of the earliest Moorish (Canaanite - Phoenicium) documents pertaining to the right, possession and inhabitation of land by blood in the Americas; describing the **Annexation of the American Continent to the Iberian Peninsula**, both, being of the present Moorish and Ancient Carthaginian Empire, is the **Bourne Stone**, in Komassakumkanit Cape Cod Bay New

England Massachussets..." Excerpt from The Consecrated Talisman 'Salmagundi' The Pi Exponent Pennatbat a Princeps Uriel – Bai Latinarius Maurusiae Hoc Publicavimus a Domus Educatio, Religionis Popularam Nostram Pro Maurisium – Americanum Societas Scientae Amplae [The Consecrated Talisman] by Prince Uriel Bey page 208.

One of the first inscriptions noted and interpreted was the so-called **Bourne Stone** of western Cape Cod, whose lettering suggests that **Carthaginian**-type people writing with the **Ibero-Punic** script may have reached the New England coast as early as 475 BCE. This Whittall-Fell collaboration was well accepted and occurred during the Golden Age of Barry Fell research.

https://www.lewrockwell.com/2015/06/no_author/the-mystery-of-cape-cods-bourne-stone/

Barry Fell claimed in his 1977 book - *America B.C.: Ancient Settlers in the New World* - that the markings are in an Iberian script and language which he translates to "**A proclamation of annexation**. **By this Hanno takes possession**.

https://en.wikipedia.org/wiki/Bourne_stone

The Phoenician Empire is the same land as biblical Canaan. Phoenician is the Greek rendering. Named so because of the purplish dye they produced. This is also the land of the Moors according to Noble Drew Ali. Therefore, it is safe to say that when Hanno lays claim circa 475-500 BC, his claim (proclamation of annexation) to the Carthaginian (Moorish or Canaanite) is before the European Christian Doctrine of Discovery authors (popes) claim.

There are numerous accounts of Muslims who were integrated within Native Indian tribes pre-Columbus, of Turkic, Moorish and African Muslims leaving colonies to live amongst the Native

Indians. There are also historical letters and colonial advertisements describing the threat to the colonies of African Muslim Slaves fleeing and integrating with the Native American Indians. There is also the case of Mahomet Weyonomonof the Mohegan tribe, who arrived in Britain in 1736 CE century to discuss the land grabs by the British.

In the 12th century Al-Idrisi reported in Nuzhat Al-Mushtaq Fi Ikhtiraq Al-Afaq (Excursion of the Longing One in Crossing Horizons), that a group of eight Muslim sailors from North Africa sailed west of Lisbon. After sailing west for more than 31 days, they landed on what must have been an island in the Caribbean. The intrepid explorers were initially imprisoned by Indians but were later released when a translator appeared who spoke Arabic

1310 CE Sultan Abu Bakari of the Mandinka kingdom of Mali sent two different fleets of ships, totalling 2,400 ships, sailing west from Africa. The fleets never returned to Africa.

There are also numerous reports of 'black skinned' Indians. For example in Honduras Columbus reported seeing Black skinned Indians. Giles Cauvet's 'Les Berberes de l'Amerique' reported that a pre-Columbian tribe in Honduras was know as the Almamys a corruption of the Mandinka word for the Arabic Imam.

The Ottoman Navy from late 14th century was one of the main navel powers, and controlled much of the Mediterranean Sea. There were many skirmishes and battles with the European nations, and as such, many Turkish sailors were imprisoned and taken to the new world. Once in the New World, these Muslim captives were assigned to slave labor on sugar plantations and in the mining operations of among other places, Cuba and Brazil.

When Santa Elena fell, its inhabitants including its converted Jews and Muslims escaped into the mountains of North Carolina.

In Eastern Tennessee in the late 1700, Jonathan Swits an English men married a Mullungeon women and utilized them in his mining operations and these dark skin individuals were known **as Mecca Indians** and they described them as being good with Silver crafts and this really comes out of Muslim Spain and Muslims were very good in that. He continues to say that they use to fall down in prayer on the ground a number of times during the day facing East.

In 1784, Tennessee governor John Seevier records an encounter with people in the Western North Carolina with **Dark reddish brown complexion** and he said that they were supposed to be of **Moorish** decent.

In 1622 CE the European colony of Jamestown was overrun by Native Americans. The African slaves did not share the same fate as the Europeans who were killed, but where instead taken and integrated into the Native

https://moorishamericannationalrepublic.com/news/the-connection-between-islam-and-native-americans/

All emphasis is mine.

www.ingramcontent.com/pod-product-compliance
Ingram Content Group UK Ltd.
Pitfield, Milton Keynes, MK11 3LW, UK
UKHW051134260726
13967UKWH00010B/3036

9 780359 577385